The Essential Hank Williams

A special book, about a very special man, written for his special fans.

By Tim Jones
With Harold McAlindon
and Richard Courtney

D1605310

ISBN: 1-886371-45-8

Cover: Charles Hooper

Special Acknowledgement

Henry and Edna Schofield

Without whose vision this book would never have been possible.

Foreword

Hank Williams is one of my heroes. No one impacted the world of country music the way he did in such a short time. There is not a singer or songwriter in country music that has not been directly or indirectly influenced by this one man. In 1996 I had the honor of portraying Hank in the musical *Lost Highway: The Music and the Legend of Hank Williams* at the world famous Ryman Auditorium in Nashville. I am also a Hank Williams historian of sorts and have studied the biographies, recordings, and pictures of Hank. I was also very honored to be asked to write the foreword for this book. These are some of the best pictures of Hank I have ever seen. In these images you will gain an insight into the man who was to become country music's greatest legend. So sit back, relax, put on an old Hank record and relive the legacy that was Hank Williams.

—Jason Petty

Introduction

No individual has impacted country music like Hank Williams. Upon being asked the question, "Which artist has influenced you and your career?" virtually every successful country recording artist or songwriter will respond with one word—Hank. Williams possessed the ability to touch our deepest feelings and emotions. For over forty years his songs have made listeners all over the world and of all ages, laugh, cry, and think. This book was created to provide Hank's fans with a wide array of information that will provide insight into why Hank Williams was who he was. The pictures in this book have never been published before. They originated from recently discovered original negatives which were taken while Williams was in the prime of his life.

During that unforgettable era, when Williams was touring as a star, when he and his entourage arrived in a town, it was an event. The entire population of the town eagerly awaited Hank. It was something people never forgot. We hope that this book rekindles some of the magic and memories.

How This Book Came To Be

In 1993, Nashville photographer Tim Jones purchased a photography studio from Henry Schofield, who had been a leading Nashville photographer for decades. Schofield's studio stood in the Hillsboro Village section of Nashville, several blocks from the world famous "Music Row". After the purchase, Jones was inventorying the studio when he stumbled across an old box labeled "Hank Williams". Little did he know the treasures he was about to discover within the dusty container. Nestled within the box were hundreds of original, never before published, photographs which had been taken while Hank was in his Golden Years. Included are several significant portraits which were taken on the very day of Hank Williams' most historic Opry appearance, June 11, 1949.

Stunned by his findings, Jones knew that other Hank Williams fans would be, too. He considered publishing a book. He was introduced by Nashville printing executive, John Craig, to Richard Courtney, founder of Eggman Publishing to determine his interest in producing a book about Hank Williams that could include some of these pictorial treasures. Courtney, a long time country music enthusiast, was enthusiastic about the prospect. He discussed it with his colleague Harold McAlindon (who as a child had won a contest, judged by Audrey Williams, to be a prospect to play Hank Williams in the movie "Your Cheatin' Heart" years ago).

So, with the help of colleague Deanie Jacobs, the three decided to compile a book for Hank Williams fans of all ages. Through this publication they have attempted to provide the reader with factual, easy to read information about the life of

The original box in which Hank Williams negatives were discovered. Note photo of Hank signing with MGM and a collection of his unique albums.

Hank Williams. Their writing has been complimented with pictures, many of which have never been seen before, that will help the reader recall the legend that brought so much to country music. The following is their tribute to Hank Williams and his fans.

Dedication:

This book is dedicated to the fans of Hank Williams . . . who
he loved so much.

Table of Contents

The Hank We Knew

The Hank We Knew

♪ Hank Williams was born on September 17, 1923, in Mount
   Olive, Alabama to Lon and Lilly Williams. His given name
   was Hiriam.

♪ Hank had a sister, Irene, and a brother who died at an early
   age.

♪ Hank's family was very transitory during his childhood as
   were many families during the Great Depression. The
   Williams were lured to follow job opportunities afforded by
   the logging industry. In later years, Hank would write the
   song, "Long Train", which was recorded on a home demo
   tape and never released. It was inspired by and dedicated to
   memories of his father.

♪ Hank's father, Lon Williams, was institutionalized in a
   Veteran's Administration hospital for nearly ten years for a
   condition which was referred to as "shell shock". This condition resulted from his participation in World War I.

♪ During Lon's hospitalization, his marriage to Lilly deterio-
   rated and Hank was raised without a true father figure.

♪ Hank's musical experiences started when he was three years old. He joined his mother on the bench as she played the organ at the Mt. Olive Baptist Church in his home town.

♪ Hank didn't begin to hone his musical skills until the age of eleven.

♪ The first instrument that Hank played in public was a jazz horn, which is similar to a kazoo. To create music, a player simply hummed into the base of the instrument.

♪ As a youth, Hank earned money shining shoes and selling peanuts.

♪ His first guitar, cost $3.50 and was ordered from the Sears and Roebuck catalog as a gift from his mother.

♪ Hank had no formal training in music or on the guitar. He was tutored and greatly influenced by a street singer named Rufus Paine, whose stage name was Tee-tot. Hank's uncanny guitar solo in "This Bucket's Got A Hole In It" was a result of Tee-tot's teachings.

♪ Many of Hank's songs reflected his personal experiences.

♪ Hank formed his first band with Hezzy Adair when Williams was thirteen. This band was the first version of the Drifting Cowboys and included Braxton Schuffert. The band played regularly on WSFA-AM in Montgomery.

♪ At the age of fourteen, Hank won an amateur night contest at the Empire Theatre in Montgomery, Alabama. He was rewarded fifteen dollars as his prize for his performance of "WPA Blues". The lyrics included

> I got a home in Montgomery
> A place I like to stay
> But I have to work for the WPA
>   And I'm dissatisfied - I'm dissatisfied.

♪ Because of his poetic ability and style, Hank was referred to as "The Hillbilly Shakespeare".

♪ Hank's first wife was Audrey Mae Sheppard. They were married in December 1944.

♪ There has been a great debate over the years as to Fred Rose's contributions to the songs he and Hank co-wrote. Many contend that Hank co-wrote. Many contend that Rose was the major contributor; however, Hank's earlier demo tapes recorded prior to his acquaintance with Rose rebut that theory. Rose's contribution in shaping Hank's earlier work is most evident.

♪ Hank could not read a note of music. However, neither could John Lennon or Paul McCartney when they wrote most of the Beatles' catalogue. It is not unusual for artist/songwriters to be unable to read music.

♪ Prior to joining the Grand Ole Opry, Hank and the Drifting Cowboys appeared frequently on the Louisiana Hayride.

♪ Hank's first records were 78 r.p.m. singles released on the Sterling label. The albums were recorded in the WSM radio studio in Nashville.

♪ Several of Hank's major hits were recorded for MGM in Cincinnati.

♪ The key ingredients to Hank's success as a songwriter were the simplicity of lyrics and melodies, and his sincerity. His innate insight into the basic psychological composition of mankind has made his work timeless.

♪ Hank made his first appearance on the Grand Ole Opry on June 11, 1949. He sang his hit song," Lovesick Blues," which had sold over three million copies. He received a standing ovation and six encores.

Fred Rose with his trademark cigar watches Hank and The Drifting Cowboys sign the MGM contract. Also on hand were key MGM executives.

Hank, Audrey, and The Drifting Cowboys (L-R) Cedric Rainwater, Audrey, Don Helms.
Standing: Jerry Rivers, Hank, Sammy Pruett.

♪ Hank's signature band, the Drifting Cowboys, was formed in July of 1949. The original Drifting Cowboys were:

Don Helms - Steel Guitar
Bob McNett - Lead Guitar
Jerry Rivers - Fiddle
Hillous Butrum - Bass

♪ On some of Hank's early recordings he used the pseudonym "Luke the Drifter".

♪ Hank's music transcended boundaries. His songs were recorded by artists ranging from Bing Crosby to Leon Russell to George Thorogood.

♪ In the early '50s, Hank had a radio show called "The Health and Happiness Show". The show was hosted by Grant Turner, the legendary Opry announcer.

♪ Hank Williams performed Fred Rose's "Blue Eyes Crying in the Rain" on the "Mother's Best Flour Radio Show" some twenty years before Willie Nelson had a hit with the song.

♪ Hank Williams had a very slight build, standing over six feet tall and weighing around 140 pounds.

Hank and Audrey's Corral located on Commerce St., (between 7th and 8th Avenue).

♪ In most of his public appearances, Hank usually wore a hat. He was balding prematurely and was rarely photographed without it.

♪ Hank's stardom lasted less than 4 years. (1949 - January 1, 1953)

♪ Hank ended his shows with, "If the good Lord's willing and the creeks don't rise, I'll see you soon."

♪ For a short while, Hank and Audrey owned "Hank and Audrey's Corral" on Commerce in downtown Nashville. Audrey relinquished ownership of the store in their divorce.

♪ Hank's original house was moved brick by brick to Music Row. The house additions, which are larger than the original construction were located on Franklin Road in Nashville.

♪ Hank's last few years were spent in discomfort due to his bad back. He was injured when he was thrown from a horse.

♪ Hank was fired from the Opry on August 11, 1952. The reason cited for his dismissal was drinking. During that time alcoholism was a misunderstood disease.

♪ Hank Williams died on January 1, 1953, at the age of 29.

♪ During his twenty-nine year lifetime, Hank recorded 129 songs.

♪ Hank's chauffeur, on the night he died, was Charles Carr who was a student at the time and needed the money for his college tuition.

♪ Hank's autopsy report officially declared that his death was caused by heart failure.

♪ The automobile in which Hank was riding when he died was a 1952 Cadillac convertible bought in North Carolina. The title number was 955627 and was registered to:

    Hank Williams
    2718 Westwood Drive
    Nashville, Tennessee

♪ He died with a scrap of paper clutched in his hand. On the paper were these words:

"We met, we lived and dear we loved, then comes that fatal day, the love that felt so dear fades far away."

♪ The title to the car was not officially issued to Hank until January 22, 1953 - three weeks after his death.

♪ The motor registration number on the car was 5266216496PE. The car is currently on display at the Hank Williams, Jr. Museum on Demonbreun Street near Music Row in Nashville.

♪ Following the death, the first Hank Williams tribute song was written by a disc jockey named Jack Cardwell. It included the lines:

Way up in West Virginia
Between midnight and dawn
A big blue car was rolling
Its wheels they hummed a song.
  Its headlights shone out through the night
To light the road so steep
  While in fact Hank Williams lay
In a deep dreamless sleep.

♪ There have been more than 700 tribute songs written and recorded about Hank Williams. The most notably are:

"Midnight in Montgomery" recorded by Alan Jackson
"The Ride" recorded by David Alan Cole
"Time Marches On" recorded by Tracy Lawrence
"Hank, You Wrote My Life" recorded by Moe Bandy
"I Don't Think Hank Done it This Way" recorded by Waylon Jennings
"If You Don't Like Hank Williams, You Can Kiss My A.." recorded by Kris Kristofferson

♪ In 1961 Hank was one of the original inductees into the Country Music Hall of Fame, along with Roy Acuff and Fred Rose. Aunt Paul Rose owned the publishing on all of Hank's songs, many of which Fred Rose was credited as a cowriter.

♪ A movie, "Your Cheatin' Heart", was made of Hank Williams. George Hamilton played the lead role. Hank Williams Jr. recorded the soundtrack.

♪ Hank's songs appealed to all audiences. During his life, he once had five of the top twelve pop songs at the time.

♪ Hank's first big break was being signed by Acuff-Rose as a songwriter. He was paid a draw of $50 a month.

28

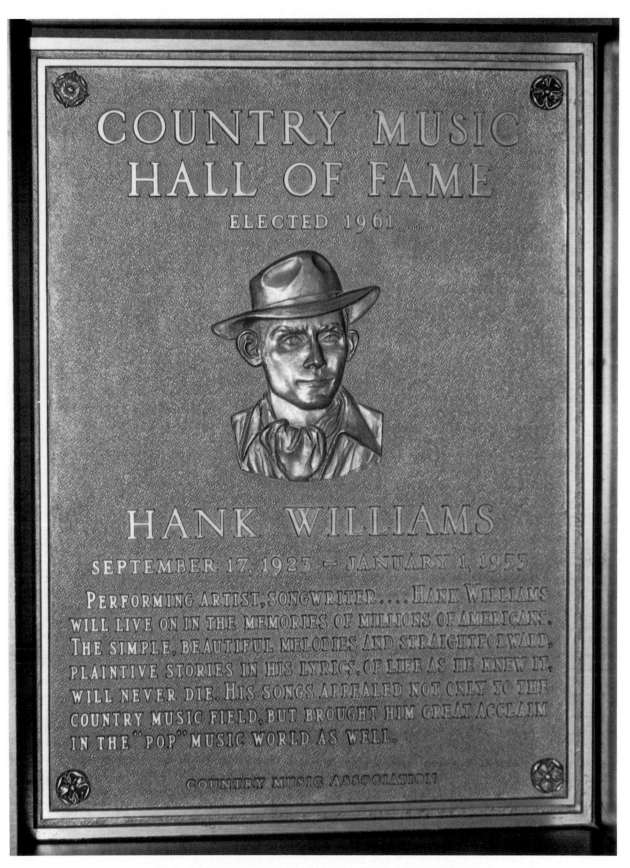

Hank's plaque in the Country Music Hall of Fame.

♪ Hank was not known for flashy rhinestone costumes. He usually wore Nudie suits, or western clothes and hand painted ties. . .always hand tooled boots.

♪ During Hank's tenure at the Opry, the word "beer" was forbidden. When Hank sung his classic, "My Bucket's Got A Hole In It—I Can't Buy No Beer", he inserted the word "milk" for the word "beer." The crowd loved it.

Grand Opening of Hank and Audrey's Corral
June 16, 1951

The opening of Hank and Audrey's Corral was a star-studded occasion. The evening was designed to launch the store as a top country entertainment venue. Not only was it an opportunity for fans to get close to their country music heros, but they witnessed one of the great country music shows of all time. Look closely at these pictures. Seven members of the Country Music Hall of Fame participated in this opening: Hank, Ernest Tubb, Red Foley, Roy Acuff, Hank Snow, Little Jimmy Dickens, and Lefty Frizzell. Also performing was George Morgan "The Candy Kid" and father of songstress Lorrie Morgan. While the Corral failed as a business venture, and was only open for a brief time, people who visited the store or witnessed their shows remember seeing the all-time country greats and hearing them at their best.

Crowd eagerly awaiting the opening.

Let's start the show!

Hank kicks it off.

The Great Roy Acuff—the "King of Country Music" performs.

Little Jimmy Dickens being interviewed by Hank.

(L-R) Ernest Tubb, Red Foley, and legendary guitarist Billy Byrd.

Hank and his guest Lefty Frizell

The Singing Ranger—Hank Snow.

(L-R) Ernest Tubb, Red Foley, and Hank

Hank and Audrey with Hank, Jr. and Lycrecia.

Quotes

I think he drank because he wanted people to pay attention to him. He wanted people to show him they loved him, and this was his way of testing them.

Ray Price

Hank Williams hardly had the luxury of a childhood; during most of his early years he had to try to be a man.

Jack Hurst

Hank did not look like himself at all in death. For one thing, his beautiful smile was missing.

"Sing A Sad Song"
by Roger M. Williams

Hank Williams, you wrote my life.

Moe Bandy

It's quite simple . . . No Hank Williams, no rock and roll.

Radney Foster

Hank Williams is the only guy I ever saw who could sit back in a chair and cross his legs and still put both feet on the floor.

Bobby Moore
Nashville Bass Player

45

Hank and Audrey

He was just a country hick like me.

Vic McAlpin
Nashville Songwriter

I never saw anybody have an effect on the Opry crowd the way he did.

Ott Devine

Hank had come out of the worst kind of poverty, the kind some stars nowadays claim to have come from and didn't.

Vic Willis

Hank—The Family Man

Audrey, Lycrecia, Hank, Jr. and Hank, Sr. pose at their house on Franklin Road.

Listening to the words of Hank's songs, it was easy to determine that at heart he was a family man.

Hank and the Drifting Cowboys look over another hit.

The Drifting Cowboys were truly part of Hank's family.

Hank (in a rare hatless photo) with Audrey and Lycrecia.

Lycrecia's 9th birthday party gathering.

Lycrecia enjoys Wesley Rose and Hank serenading her at her birthday party.

Audrey Williams

Lycrecia Williams

Hank, Sr. and Bocephus

That Magical Night

On the show that night were Red Foley, Minnie Pearl, Eddie Arnold, Roy Acuff, and Dr. Lew Childre.

That Magical Night

Countless stories have been told about Hank Williams' first appearance at the Grand Ole Opry on June 11, 1949 and those in the audience agree about one thing: There hasn't been a night like it at the Opry before or since.

To recapture that evening you must recall that Hank Williams was not widely known. He had recorded under the name of "Luke The Drifter" and only recently had hit the charts with his classic "Lovesick Blues". Fans who attended the Ryman Auditorium for an Opry appearance can remember how intimate the setting was. The audience was practically on top of the performers. The shows were fairly tight due to the large number of performers who appeared on each show.

That eventful night the show featured such stars as Roy Acuff, Red Foley, and Minnie Pearl. New artists were given a one-song guest shot. When Hank was introduced to the audience he received only polite applause for there was no name recognition.

As he sang the first words of "Love Sick Blues," the audience erupted, and his voice lost in the roar, as the crowd rose as one. Hank responded, blushing that soon-to-be-famous smile.

Hank received another standing ovation and had to do a half dozen encores. Red Foley had to literally plead with the audience to let the show continue.

The photographs on the following pages were taken on the day of that historic appearance.

The Hank Williams Show

The Hank Williams Show

In addition to his road shows, Hank had a radio program called "The Health and Happiness Show". This program also featured the Drifting Cowboys, Audrey Williams, and famed Opry announcer, the late Grant Turner. Despite the ups and downs of his marriage, Audrey was truly the love of his life. The Drifting Cowboys created a sound that was unique and easily identifiable on any of Hank's great records.

Grant Turner for many years was synonymous with the Grand Ole Opry and country music. You only have to look at the expressions of the two faces in these photographs to see the very special relationship that they had.

Duck Head Overalls was a perfect sponsor for Hank Williams because his appeal to hard working people was so strong and rooted in his personal history. People could identify wih the problems that Hank wrote and sang about.

While Miss Audrey was a performer in her own right, she never acheived stardom and for the most part her claim to fame was being the wife of Hank Williams.

Hank with music executives. To Hank's right is George Morgan.

Hank promoting work clothes for Duck Head.

"Your're on, Hank!"

Why We Loved
Hank Williams

On the Road With Hank

Don Helms worked with Hank Williams for years as his steel guitar player. His distinctive style was an important part of the "Hank Williams Sound". The sounds he created were greatly respected by steel guitar players in his generation and the generations that followed. He is so revered by his colleagues that he was elected to the Steel Guitar Hall of Fame in St. Louis, Missouri in1984. In addition to being a musician, he was one of Hank's closest personal friends. He said, "I spent more time hunting and fishing with Hank than I did playing music."

When the Hank Williams Show was on the road they often stayed in nice hotels, such as, The Book Cadillac in Detroit and the Adolphus Hotel in Dallas. While the accommodations were posh, transport to and from the shows was another story. In those days, country music stars did not have buses. The band would car pool to their appearances with the instruments visible to the general public. As they motored on their way, the trunks and the car tops would be loaded down, and the roof of the car was often reserved for the stand-up bass fiddle.

According to Don Helms, "When it rained the bass fiddle had to be put inside the car." "Sometimes, " he said, "if it rained for several days, people in the back seat would not be able to talk to each other for an entire trip because they were separated by a huge bass fiddle."

Life on the road can bring out the worst in a person. Especially when times were tough.

According to Don, Hank Williams never acted like a

"boss", although the band members knew he certainly was the leader. "We were just five guys in a car or five guys on stage," Helms recalled.

Hank possessed a marvelously dry sense of humor and could "take it" as well as he could dole it out, according to the Drifting Cowboys. Long road trips can spawn a unique sense of humor among creative musicians forced to exist in such close quarters. Hank was once described by a band member as "so skinny he could change clothes in a shotgun and never get any powder on him".

While in town, the Cowboys, with Hank in tow all ate in the same place and they loved large breakfasts. Ham and eggs, hash browns, toast, sausage, red-eye gravy and coffee were standard meals for Hank and his band. One of Hank's favorite eateries was The Beacon which was on Highway 100 in Nashville.

They were paid good money for those days but Hank's biggest payday was $1,000 a day (and that included the band). Because of his meager beginnings he was very proud of his accomplishments and his possessions. He had a particular fancy for nice cars. Because he liked "the best", he also provided the quality stage costumes for the Drifting Cowboys when he reached stardom.

When asked how Hank would feel about the new show "The Lost Highway: The Legend of Hank Williams Music". Don Helms responded, "Hank would be proud to know that people still remember him and are enjoying his music."

On the road Hank and the Drifting Cowboys were frequently packaged with Cowboy Copas and Little Jimmy Dickens or Minnie Pearl and Ernest Tubb. He appeared on several TV shows but only his appearance on Kate Smith where he sang, "Hey Good Lookin'" has been saved.

When coming back off of the road, Hank and the Drifting Cowboys would pause near the Nashville airport and Hank would say "we must be near Montgomery because I saw the light." He was referring to the beacon to guide incoming planes. That is probably where he got the line, "I saw the light" for his great song of the same name.

Hank loved Ernest Tubb and Roy Acuff as artists and would frequently try to emulate them. On one occasion Fred Rose suggested that Hank get "somewhere in between them in style". That's when Hank's personal style began to emerge. On the road he usually played a Martin guitar although occasionally he would use a Gibson.

Hank Williams' alcoholism did not interfere with his dedication to his profession. Don Helms stated, "Hank was stone sober 95% of the time and his writings were done while he was sober."

He wore expensive suits created by Nudie, with a western look, his trademark white hat was a Stetson, along with hand-painted ties.

Being on the road with Hank Williams was special. He had a genuine love affair with his fans. One show in a park in Pennsylvania, thousands of people showed up for a show. Suddenly a tremendous storm erupted. The band scurried behind the overhang to protect themselves. To everyone's surprise the audience didn't move. They didn't run to their cars, or get under umbrellas, they just sat there. Hank was moved. He walked back on stage and announced "if you're willing to sit in this rain to see me, I'm willing to stand in the rain and sing for you." With a $5,000 Martin guitar and expensive suit, Hank sung solo for his fans in that tremendous downpour. That epitomizes why people loved Hank Williams.

Hank was very sensitive about taking the name of the Lord in vain. He took a box and cut a slot on top of it. He announced to his band that each would have to put 25 cents in the box every time they cursed or used profanity. One day Hank was putting some change in the box and he rolled up a dollar to try to insert it in the slot. When asked what he was doing, he answered, "I feel three or four coming".

Hank was balding. One day he was being interviewed for a role in an MGM movie, "Small Town Girl". He was asked to

One of Hank's favorite hand-painted ties.

turn around so the movie executives could get a good look at him. As usual he was wearing his white hat. He was asked, "Do you have any hair?" Hank answered, "Yes, sir, I have a whole drawer full of it".

The whole gang for Duck Head.

On the Road With Hank

Don Helms worked with Hank Williams for years as his steel guitar player. His distinctive style was an important part of the "Hank Williams Sound". The sounds he created were greatly respected by steel guitar players in his generation and the generations that followed. He is so revered by his colleagues that he was elected to the Steel Guitar Hall of Fame in St. Louis, Missouri in1984. In addition to being a musician, he was one of Hank's closest personal friends. He said, "I spent more time hunting and fishing with Hank than I did playing music."

When the Hank Williams Show was on the road they often stayed in nice hotels, such as, The Book Cadillac in Detroit and the Adolphus Hotel in Dallas. While the accommodations were posh, transport to and from the shows was another story. In those days, country music stars did not have buses. The band would car pool to their appearances with the instruments visible to the general public. As they motored on their way, the trunks and the car tops would be loaded down, and the roof of the car was often reserved for the stand-up bass fiddle.

According to Don Helms, "When it rained the bass fiddle had to be put inside the car." "Sometimes, " he said, "if it rained for several days, people in the back seat would not be able to talk to each other for an entire trip because they were separated by a huge bass fiddle."

Life on the road can bring out the worst in a person. Especially when times were tough.

According to Don, Hank Williams never acted like a

"boss", although the band members knew he certainly was the leader. "We were just five guys in a car or five guys on stage," Helms recalled.

Hank possessed a marvelously dry sense of humor and could "take it" as well as he could dole it out, according to the Drifting Cowboys. Long road trips can spawn a unique sense of humor among creative musicians forced to exist in such close quarters. Hank was once described by a band member as "so skinny he could change clothes in a shotgun and never get any powder on him".

While in town, the Cowboys, with Hank in tow all ate in the same place and they loved large breakfasts. Ham and eggs, hash browns, toast, sausage, red-eye gravy and coffee were standard meals for Hank and his band. One of Hank's favorite eateries was The Beacon which was on Highway 100 in Nashville.

They were paid good money for those days but Hank's biggest payday was $1,000 a day (and that included the band). Because of his meager beginnings he was very proud of his accomplishments and his possessions. He had a particular fancy for nice cars. Because he liked "the best", he also provided the quality stage costumes for the Drifting Cowboys when he reached stardom.

When asked how Hank would feel about the new show "The Lost Highway: The Legend of Hank Williams Music". Don Helms responded, "Hank would be proud to know that people still remember him and are enjoying his music."

On the road Hank and the Drifting Cowboys were frequently packaged with Cowboy Copas and Little Jimmy Dickens or Minnie Pearl and Ernest Tubb. He appeared on several TV shows but only his appearance on Kate Smith where he sang, "Hey Good Lookin'" has been saved.

When coming back off of the road, Hank and the Drifting Cowboys would pause near the Nashville airport and Hank would say "we must be near Montgomery because I saw the light." He was referring to the beacon to guide incoming planes. That is probably where he got the line, "I saw the light" for his great song of the same name.

Hank loved Ernest Tubb and Roy Acuff as artists and would frequently try to emulate them. On one occasion Fred Rose suggested that Hank get "somewhere in between them in style". That's when Hank's personal style began to emerge. On the road he usually played a Martin guitar although occasionally he would use a Gibson.

Hank Williams' alcoholism did not interfere with his dedication to his profession. Don Helms stated, "Hank was stone sober 95% of the time and his writings were done while he was sober."

He wore expensive suits created by Nudie, with a western look, his trademark white hat was a Stetson, along with hand-painted ties.

Being on the road with Hank Williams was special. He had a genuine love affair with his fans. One show in a park in Pennsylvania, thousands of people showed up for a show. Suddenly a tremendous storm erupted. The band scurried behind the overhang to protect themselves. To everyone's surprise the audience didn't move. They didn't run to their cars, or get under umbrellas, they just sat there. Hank was moved. He walked back on stage and announced "if you're willing to sit in this rain to see me, I'm willing to stand in the rain and sing for you." With a $5,000 Martin guitar and expensive suit, Hank sung solo for his fans in that tremendous downpour. That epitomizes why people loved Hank Williams.

Hank was very sensitive about taking the name of the Lord in vain. He took a box and cut a slot on top of it. He announced to his band that each would have to put 25 cents in the box every time they cursed or used profanity. One day Hank was putting some change in the box and he rolled up a dollar to try to insert it in the slot. When asked what he was doing, he answered, "I feel three or four coming".

Hank was balding. One day he was being interviewed for a role in an MGM movie, "Small Town Girl". He was asked to

One of Hank's favorite hand-painted ties.

turn around so the movie executives could get a good look at him. As usual he was wearing his white hat. He was asked, "Do you have any hair?" Hank answered, "Yes, sir, I have a whole drawer full of it".

The whole gang for Duck Head.

The Stamp

The following passage was exerpted from the book, *Songs That Changed Our Lives*, by Bruce Burch published by Eggman Publishing, Inc.

The Stamp

A young boy named Beecher O'Quinn, Jr., better known as Junior, was nine years old when Hank Williams passed away. He remembers the day well. But it was not until five years later on New Year's Day in 1958 that the impact of Hank Williams' life, death, and music made its mark on young Junior.

A disc jockey named Curly White was hosting what had become an annual New Year's Day tradition on country radio stations across the nation--a Hank Williams tribute. Junior was sitting in the front seat of his older brother's 1948 Chevrolet when he was struck by the mournful music coming from the radio. As he now recalls:

"The song that really grabbed my attention was Mansion on the Hill. I thought it was the most beautiful song that I had ever heard--the music, the voice, and the words seemed to go together perfectly. Mansion on the Hill is still my all-time favorite Hank Williams song. The radio tribute lasted around two hours. I almost ran my brother's car battery down--and the more I listened, the more fascinated I became. At that time, of course, I didn't even know what Hank looked like. From the sincerety of his voice, however, I thought he sounded like a man in his late fifties. Later, I was surprised to learn that he was just a little more than 29 years of age at the time of his death."

Junior began to collect Hank Williams records and played them on the small record player he shared with his two younger sisters. He also began collecting pictures, stories, magazine articles, books, and virtually anything he could find about Hank. As he grew up and his life went on, Junior continued to be a big fan of Hank Williams, Sr.

But in November of 1990, Junior became more than just another fan. He began a campaign that will forever stand as a tribute to the legendary performer.

As Junior was checking his mail at the post office one morning, he noticed a clipboard containing information about the different commemorative stamps the postal service had begun to issue. He saw the various themes and people that were due to appear on upcoming stamps, and thought to himself that if anybody deserved such an honor, it was Hank Williams.

He went home that night and couldn't sleep from thinking about his idea. He had no knowledge of how to initiate the project, but by the next day he had decided that it was his mission. (At that time he also had no knowledge that a decade earlier a group of fans had tried unsuccessfully to accomplish the same task).

Junior checked with the local postmaster and was given the address of the Citizens Stamp Advisory Committee in Washington, D.C. The next day he wrote a letter to the committee and placed Hank's name in nomination.

Junior didn't stop there. He also went to the library and looked up the names and addresses of the various governors, U.S. congressmen, and senators. He sent them all letters asking for their support in his effort.

In addition, he wrote Merle Kilgore, Hank Williams, Jr.'s, manager, to receive their blessing on the project. After Merle and Hank, Jr. received assurances that Junior's motives for pursuing this project were out of love and respect for Hank, Sr., they supported him wholeheartedly.

Before it was over, some 7,000 pieces of mail had been sent out. Junior ended up receiving the support of 22 governors (including then-Arkansas governor Bill Clinton), 10 U.S. senators, 8 U.S. respresentatives, and 28 mayors. With the help of many people, he was able to get the signatures of a host of country stars on his petitions, including Charlie Pride (who also wrote a letter of support), Ray Price, Boxcar Willie, Kitty Wells, Mel Tillis, Mickey Gilley, the Oak Ridge Boys, Minnie Pearl . . . and the list goes on and on.

Junior was, in fact, informed that the postal service got more letters about Hank's stamp than they received for the highly publicized Elvis commemorative stamp.

Nearly three years passed as Junior O'Quinn continued working on the project. Finally, at country music's Fan Fair on

June 9, 1993, his dream became a reality. Marvin Runyon, the Postmaster General of the United States, along with Hank Williams, Jr., unveiled the Hank Williams, Sr. Commemorative Postage Stamp on the stage in front of thousands of Fan Fair attendees.

Junior O'Quinn stood and watched with pride—not because of something he had accomplished, but because the accomplishments of his hero were finally being recognized.

Hank Williams Commemorative Stamp

The "Two Faced Preacher" Controversy

The "Two Faced Preacher" Controversy

When Hank had his own radio show on WSFA in Montgomery, he sang a song he had written which was entitled "Two Faced Preacher." In it he condemned clergy who failed to practice what they preached. It was his first brush with controversy.

After performing the song, the radio station received several telephone calls from irate listeners protesting the content of the song. Montgomery was rooted deeply in the Bible Belt. The conservative listenership of the station were unaccustomed, and uncomfortable, hearing such criticism of men of the cloth.

Jack Loftin, a fourteen year-old guitar student, was a guest on the Saturday show when one listener called in. Bill Smith, the disc jockey, entered the studio from the control room to inform Hank of the complaints he was receiving. Loftin recalled, "Hank turned to the microphone and said, 'If you don't like what I'm singing, take a look at that little knob you used to turn your radio on...Well, that same little knob will turn it off, too.'"

The next Monday, Hank received a petition signed by twenty-two preachers imploring him not to perform the song on the air. Hank's week day show was at 6:30 a.m. and he felt most of the clergy would still be slumbering at that time of day. Therefore, he waited for his Saturday show which aired at 11:30 a.m. to perform the song again.

He met the same criticism following his rendition of "The Two Faced Preacher." The following Monday the twenty-two man constituency of clergy donated one dollar apiece to their cause. Hank accepted the twenty-two dollars as a fee in return for his promise to never perform the song again. It was the first, and last time that Hank Williams was paid not to sing.

Hank lived by his word. He offered the song to Jack Loftin, told him he could have the rights to the song, to use as he wished. Loftin's release of the song was April of 1996—fifty-three years after his mentor presented it to him.

Hank signing with MGM

Guitar Instruction's Loss
Is Country Music's Gain

Guitar Instruction's Loss Is Country Music's Gain

In 1943, Jack Loftin was a thirteen year-old school boy with
ambitions of country music stardom. He lived on a farm several miles outside Montgomery with his family. Jack's father
shared his son's aspirations and wanted to support him in any
way possible.

Being a fan of country music himself, the elder Loftin
would often listen to WSFA radio in nearby Montgomery. The
station had a strong signal and reached all of Southern
Alabama as well as parts of Georgia and Mississippi. Mr.
Loftin was a part-time cab driver in Montgomery. One day his
fare was a recognizable figure who was a regular on WSFA -
Hank Williams.

The cabby took advantage of his captive audience of one
and asked Hank if he would teach his son to play the guitar.
Williams responded that he would indeed for the sum of one
dollar per lesson. The lesson would take place on any
Wednesday, which was Hank's only day off.

Jack's father was greatly excited, and felt certain that stardom was imminent for young Jack. Hank then offered some
sagely advice which brought the gloating father back to earth.
Hank said if he was Mr. Loftin, he would take his son's guitar
and wrap it around a tree.

Jack Loftin took approximately thirty lessons from Hank
over a period of two years. His instructional style was
unorthodox and interesting.

He refused to allow Jack to keep time by patting his foot.

Hank, Sr. sings to Hank, Jr.

He insisted that his student use his neck, shoulders, and head in order to keep time. If Williams noticed Loftin tapping time, Loftin would feel the sole of Hank's boot crash down upon his tapping toes. Loftin would usually develop a crick in his neck while practicing or performing.

After developing one such crick, Loftin remarked that he noticed Hank tapped his foot to keep time. Williams sternly reminded him of their respective roles - he the teacher, Loftin the student. He instructed Loftin to do as his teacher said, not as his teacher did.

Following one lesson, Hank commented that he had noticed Jack watched his fingers as he changed chords. Williams informed his student that they would work on that during the next lesson. They did.

The lesson took place in Hank's bedroom in the upstairs of his mother's boarding house which was located in Montgomery. The first floor housed a barber shop and a coffee house. The bedroom was very stark, void of decoration, consisting of a wardrobe, a bed, and a bedstead. Over the bed hung a picture of Miss Lillie, Hank's mother.

In order to teach Jack to play his instrument in a showmanly fashion, Hank suggested that Jack look at the picture of Miss Lillie as he played. From time to time, Loftin would regress to his old habits and sneak a peek at his fingers as he changed chords.

"I told you to look at Mama!" Hank reprimanded each time.

Loftin is of the opinion that Hank's song "Old and Faded Picture on the Wall" was inspired by the portrait. Perhaps, it was written as Hank himself practiced his guitar playing.

The emphasis of Hank's guitar instruction reflected his personal philosophy, theory, and strength - rhythm. He realized the driving force behind the music was its rhythm and attempted to pass that along to Jack.

Loftin appreciated the attention to the detail of the rhythm, but also yearned to learn some runs and a "hot lick" or two.

Bocephus returns the favor.

As they began their lesson one Wednesday afternoon, Hank invited Jack to play what he had practiced since their last lesson.

Loftin had spent hours learning the guitar run featured on Ernest Tubb's "Walking the Floor." He played it for Williams hoping to impress him. Following his flawless performance, the beaming eyes of the pupil met the glaring eye of the master.

"Who the hell taught you that?" Williams admonished.

"The guy next door?"

"Are you taking lessons from 'the guy next door' or me?" he asked angrily.

"You?" Loftin managed to utter.

"No more runs. No licks. Rhythm! Rhythm!" Hank demanded.

Rhythm it was. Soon Loftin became accomplished enough that Hank thought Jack was ready to perform on WSFA. They spent all afternoon one Wednesday working on the song "Cowboy Jack," performing it six or eight times.

Loftin stayed up all night as eagerness and anxiety robbed him of sleep. Hank introduced Jack by saying "This is the boy I've been teaching to play the guitar. By the way, if anyone wants to learn to play the guitar, give me a call at the station."

Was Williams' entrepreneurial spirit showing through or was he proud of his student? Hank was known for his ability to make a dollar. Even during the depression, he made money shining shoes and selling peanuts. Whatever the case the lessons continued.

As the lessons went on Hank became more comfortable with Jack. One day Jack handed Hank his dollar and Hank returned it to him along with a different type of instruction. He told Loftin that there was a beer cooler under the counter in the coffee house downstairs. Williams ordered him to go down and purchase five Falstaff beers.

The fifteen year-old Loftin, his heart full of fear, obeyed and returned with the goods. This exercise was repeated sev-

eral times in the weeks ahead. Jack not only became less fear-
ful of the task, but soon grew to enjoy it as it made for a more
enthusiastic lecturer and often led to a two hour lesson.

The Ride

Hank and executive Harry Stone

The Ride

In late 1952 Hank seemed to be getting his life together. Some people thought he had gained some weight and was looking better than he had in years. His career, which had seen its ups and downs, seemed poised for another surge. He was booked for shows on New Year's Eve in Charleston, West Virginia and New Year's Day in Canton, Ohio. Even talks of returning to the Opry were rumored.

The throngs were ready to welcome Hank back. He had intended to fly to Canton but because of weather problems he had to change his plans. Finding a driver to make the trek from Montgomery, Alabama, to Canton, Ohio was not an easy task.

He was able to enlist the aid of an Auburn University student, Charles Carr, who needed tuition money for the upcoming semester. His father owned a cab company in Montgomery and he made the arrangements for his teenage son to drive the ailing superstar to the shows.

The weather conditions were horrible with freezing rain, wind, and snow. Hank had originally intended to drive to Knoxville and then fly to Cincinnati, however, all flights had been cancelled. Therefore, Hank was unable to reach the show in Charleston and he arranged to meet the Drifting Cowboys in Canton. They would appear on the New Year's Show along with Hankshaw Hawkins, Homer and Jethro, The Webb Sisters and Autry Inman.

The day prior the scheduled performance, Hank and young Carr left to make the trip to the show. Hank was in agony. He had experienced excruciating pain from a back ailment for the last few years. Many conject that he may have suffered from spina bifada. He tried to sleep in the back seat in

order to elude the pain. He spent most of the trip in uneasy slumber and they stopped near Knoxville for an injection of pain killer. It was not unusual for him to sleep in the back seat as he frequently would spend his travel time writing songs, working on ideas for his show, or catching up on sleep that he had lost due to his busy schedule.

As the ride continued, a patrolman stopped Charles Carr. During the verbal exchange with Mr. Carr, the officer asked, "What's wrong with your friend in the back seat?"

"Oh, he's just sleeping." Carr answered.

"He looks dead to me," the patrolman observed.

The Cadillac pulled away and continued en route to Canton. The policeman's observations haunted Charles Carr. He pulled into a service station in Oak Hill, Virginia and reached into the back seat to awaken Hank. Hank was dead.

When word got to Canton, the audience and the artists were devastated. As the announcement was made, the audience stood and sang one of Hank's classics, "I Saw The Light".

People wept openly and mourned the loss of country music's greatest star. The car in which Hank died is now on display in the Hank Williams, Jr. Museum on Music Row. His music still echoes in the hearts and minds of his millions of fans.

The Hank Williams gravesite in Montgomery, Alabama.

The Beginning

Hank Williams' shockingly sudden death in 1953 caused his many fans to pause and reflect on his music. This is as it was, and as it would have been expected to be. Ironically, his stature as a legend began to grow almost immediately, catapulting Hank Williams into a yet unparalleled country stardom that continues to grow to this day. Throughout America, devastated fans who loved him and his music poured out their emotion. Grief, openly expressed, was commonplace, as Hank Williams' music filled the airways in America's diners, bars and automobiles.

Two of Williams' greatest hits, "Your Cheatin' Heart" and "Kaw-Liga" were released after his death. The word and music was spread and the appeal of Hank Williams proved contagious. It became apparent that Hank Williams' music was not simply transmitted by radios, records, and sheet music. It was locked in the hearts and minds of a multitude of fans. Not surprisingly, his songs are still popular, and his place at the highest peak in country music remains. Hank Williams achieved this by reflecting the lives of each listener in the lyrics of his hits. Through his music, people learned to understand each other, they learned to understand themselves, and his haunting, soulful tone masterfully reached and inevitably affected each person.

Virtually every major artist today has been influenced by Hank Williams. And they, in turn, will influence the stars of tomorrow. The chain of classics continues to grow, and Hank Williams' music is its single most important link. How long will the legend of Hank Williams continue? As long as there is heartache, loneliness, inspiration, beauty, jealousy, and love. Human emotion in its most raw state is captured through each Hank Williams song. Each one reverberates deeply and personally in the hearts of forever growing numbers of Hank Williams fans.

Thank you, Hank

Special Thanks To

Don Helms (Drifting Cowboy)
Mike Hyland-Gaylord Entertainment
Country Jack Loftin
Matt Lindsey
Bruce Burch
Beecher O'Quinn
Radney Foster
Deanie Jacobs
Mike Delevante
Jason Petty
Barbara Watts
Charles Hooper
Mike Walker
Beth Seigenthaler
Currey Copple
Kay McGhee